The Ra

Contents	Page
What is a rainforest?	2-3
Jungle	4-5
Canopy	6
Forest floor	7
Birds	8
Monkeys	9
Frogs, bats, and butterflies	10
Snakes	11
Tigers and jaguars	12-13
People	14-15
Rainforests for the world	16

written by John Lockyer

1

rainforest

Rainforests are very, very old. They have been on Earth for millions of years.

A rainforest is full of trees, plants, flowers, and animals. It rains there on most days.

jungle

Rainforests in hot countries are warm and wet all year. Sometimes they are called jungles.

4

More kinds of animals and plants live in the rainforests than anywhere else in the world.

canopy

Trees in a rainforest can be as high as a tall building. The tops of the tall trees make a canopy like a roof.

The canopy makes the floor of the forest very dark.
Snails and spiders and insects live there in all kinds of plants.

scarlet macaw

Many kinds of birds live in the
canopy of the rainforest.
They build nests in the branches.
Their food is insects and seeds.

red howler monkey

Monkeys swing from branches
and vines high in the canopy.
They like to eat fruit and nuts.

Little tree frogs hop along the branches, and bright butterflies live there, too. Bats fly quietly at night.

red-eyed tree frog

Snakes are hard to see as they slide along rainforest trees.

green python

tiger

The biggest hunters on the forest floor are hungry tigers and jaguars.

Jaguars can climb trees, and they like to hunt at night.

Some people live in the rainforest. Their homes are huts, and they use canoes to travel on the rivers. They catch fish and hunt animals.

hut

Rainforest children do not go to school, but they have to learn all about life in the rainforest.

chameleon

Rainforests are full of life.
The world needs its rainforests.